THE
PAINTED
BED

THE
PAINTED
BED

Donald Hall

A MARINER BOOK
HOUGHTON MIFFLIN COMPANY
Boston   New York

First Mariner Books edition 2003

Copyright © 2002 by Donald Hall

Visit our Web site: www.houghtonmifflinbooks.com.

Book design by Anne Chalmers
Typeface: Filosophia © Emigré

Printed in the United States of America

QUM 10 9 8 7 6 5 4 3 2 1

Library of Congress Cataloging-in-Publication Data
and acknowledgments appear on page 89.

The true subject of poetry

is the death of the beloved.

—Faiz Ahmed Faiz

Joyce

Caroline

Alice

Contents

THE PAINTED BED

"Even when I danced erect
by the Nile's garden
I constructed Necropolis.

Ten million fellaheen cells
of my body floated stones
to establish a white museum."

Grisly, foul, and terrific
is the speech of bones,
thighs and arms slackened

into desiccated sacs of flesh
hanging from an armature
where muscle was, and fat.

"I lie on the painted bed
diminishing, concentrated
on the journey I undertake

to repose without pain
in the palace of darkness,
my body beside your body."

I
KILL THE DAY

Work, love, build a house, and die.

—*The One Day*

KILL THE DAY

When she died it was as if his car accelerated
off the pier's end and zoomed upward over death water
for a year without gaining or losing altitude,
then plunged to the bottom of the sea where his corpse
lay twisted in a honeycomb of steel, still dreaming
awake, as dead as she was but conscious still.
There is nothing so selfish as misery nor so boring,
and depression is devoted only to its own practice.
Mourning resembles melancholia precisely except
that melancholy adds self-loathing to stuporous sorrow

and turns away from the dead its exclusive attention.
Mania is melancholy reversed. Bereavement, loss,
and guilt provide excitement for conversion
to dysphoria, murderous rage, and unsleeping joy.
When he rose from the painted bed, he alternated or cycled
from dedicated hatred through gaiety and inflation
to the vacancy of breathing in-and-out, in-and-out.
He awakened daily to the prospect of nothingness
in the day's house that like all houses was mortuary.
He slept on the fornicating bed of the last breath.

He closed her eyes in the noon of her middle life;
he no longer cut and pruned for her admiration;
he worked for the praise of women and they died.
For months after her chest went still, he nightmared
that she had left him for another man. Everything

became its opposite and returned to itself.
As the second summer of her death approached him,
goldfinches flew at her feeder like daffodils
with wings and he could no longer tell her so.
Her absence could no longer be written to.

He emptied her shelves, dressers, and closets,
stacking rings and bracelets, pendants and necklaces.
He bundled sweaters and jeans, brassieres and blouses,
scarves and nightgowns and suits and summer dresses
and mailed them to Rosie's Place for indigent women.
For decades a man and a woman living together
learned each other for pleasure, giving and taking,
studying every other day predictable ecstasy
secure without secrecy or adventure, without romance,
without anxiety or jealousy, without content

except for the immaculate sexual content of sex.
The toad sat still for the toad's astounding moment,
but the day wasted whatever lived for the day
and the only useful desire obliterates desire.
Now the one day extended into multiple encounters
with loneliness that could not endure a visitor.
Machinery corroded in the barn no longer entered,
and no smoke rose from the two opposite chimneys.
It is naïve to complain over death and abandonment,
and the language of houses praised only itself.

Bone's Orchard bragged of breakfast and work, church
with neighbors on Sunday, gardening, the pond, and love

in the afternoon. The day ignored that it undertook
mere interruption on the trudge to fathomless loss.
"The days you work," said O'Keeffe, "are the best days."
Work without love is idle, idleness doing its job
for the velvet approbation of kings and presidents
without art's purpose to excite a lover's pleasure.
He turned into the ash heap damp in the Glenwood,
the burnt shape and constitution of wretchedness

in his ludicrous rage that things are as they are.
When she died, at first the outline of absence defined
a presence that disappeared. He wept for the body
he could no longer reach to touch in bed on waking.
He wept for her silver thimble. He wept when the dog
brought him a slipper that smelled of her still.
In another summer, her pheromones diminished.
The negative space of her body dwindled as she receded
deeper into the ground, smaller and fainter each day,
dried out, shrunken, separated from the news of the day.

When the coffee cup broke, when her yellow bathrobe
departed the bathroom door, when the address book
in her hand altered itself into scratchings-out,
he dreaded an adventure of self-hatred accomplished
by the finger or toe of an old man alone without
an onion to eat between slices of store-bought bread.
There was nothing to do, and nothing required doing.
Her vanishing constructed a blue synagogue
in a universe without solace or a task for doing.
He imagined that on shelves at his workroom's end

lay stacked two hundred and sixty-seven tiny
corpses, bodies of her body, porcelain mannequins.
In this dream or story he had neglected to bury them;
it was something still to do, something to be done.
In the second year, into the third and fourth years,
she died again and again, she died by receding
while he recited each day the stanzas of her dying:
He watched her chest go still; he closed her eyes.
Without birthdays, she remained her age at death.
The figurine broke that clutched its fists

as she did dying. In the pantry there were cans
and boxes and jars she bought in the supermarket
seven years ago. He walked through the vacancies,
burying her again. He had imagined an old man
alone in this white house, looking in the mirror.
Looking in the mirror now, he was old and alone.
He felt solitude's relief and intolerably lonely.
He envied whatever felt nothing: He envied oak
sills and the green hill rising and the boulder
by the side of the road and his dead love rotting

in her best white dress inside Vermont hardwood.
It was useful to set his name on her black granite,
but imminent or eventual cellular junction provided
the comfort of stone: to keep her safe beside him.
Visions of pleasure departed when she departed.
The condition of contentment or satisfaction
remains unattainable because of affect's agreement:
Whatever the measure of joy in the day's day,

6

no pleasure carries with it one part in ten million
of agony's vastation in loss and abandonment.

Therefore the condition of being alive is intolerable,
with no reason for endurance except that DNA
continues itself in order to continue itself.
Agreeing to love each other, they perfected a system:
Love is the exchange of a double narcissism,
agreement of twin surrender, the weapons laid by,
the treaty enforced by habitual daily negotiation.
What would he do if he could do what he wanted?
The day prevented him from doing what he wanted.
Now he woke each morning wretched with morning's

regret that he woke. He woke looking forward
to a nap, to a cigarette, to supper, to port measured,
to sleep blessed sleep on the permanent painted bed
of death: Sleep, rage, kill the day, and die.
When she died, he died also. For the first year
his immediate grief confused him into feeling alive.
He endured the grief of a two-month love affair.
When women angry and free generously visited
the frenzy of his erotic grief, melancholia
became ecstasy, then sank under successful dirt.

Without prospect or purpose, who dares to love meat
that will putrefy? He rejoiced that he was meat.
How many times will he die in his own lifetime?
When TWA 800 blew out of the sky, his heart ascended
and exploded in gratitude, finding itself embodied

and broken as fragments scattering into water.
Then little green testicles dropped from the oaks
on New Canada Road again, another August of death,
and autumn McIntoshes rotted on the dwarf trees
already pecked by the loathsome birds of July.

Each day identified itself as a passage to elsewhere,
which was a passage to elsewhere and to elsewhere.
What did she look like now? Dried and slackening maybe.
Do the worms eat her? He supposed that they ate her.
Now he dreamed again of her thick and lavish hair,
of her lush body wetting and loosening beside him.
He remembered ordinary fucking that shone like the sun
in their household solar system, brighter than Jesus,
than poetry, than their orchard under the mountain—
the crossing place of bodies that regarded each other

with more devotion the more they approached her death
until they were singular, gazing speechless together
while she vanished into open eyes staring all night.
In the day's crush and tangle of melted nails,
collapsed foundation stones, and adze-trimmed beams,
the widower alone glimpsed the beekeeper's mask
in high summer as it approached the day they built,
now fallen apart with bark still on its beams,
nine layers of wallpaper over the dry laths—
always ending, no other ending, in dead eyes open.

II
DEATHWORK

1

The After Life

It took two hours
for the Visiting Nurse
to arrive and certify
that Jane was dead.
It took another hour
for Marion and Charlie
to come from Chadwick's
with the van, the canvas
stretcher, and the gurney.
When one day he saw her
walking Gussie on New Canada
Road, or heard her voice
calling him "Perkins!"
across a parking lot,
he had confirmed her death
with his eyes,
his fingers, and his lips.

*

The afternoon Jane died,
six-year-old Allison and he
pushed through the toolshed
to stroll outside
and look at the daffodils,
but stopped short to see
the crayoned cardboard

tacked over the freezer
with capital letters in blues,
reds, and greens: WELCOME
BACK JANE FROM SEATTLE!

*

As he started up-town
to see her laid out
in her white salwar kameez,
he worried how she would look,
made up. Halfway there,
he U-turned; he had
forgotten to wear his glasses.

*

Calling Hours: Chadwick's,
where we saw the last
of Kate, Lucy, Jack, and half
the village. The neighbors
filed past Jane. Dick came inside
while Nan sat propped in the car,
and he went out to kiss Nan's
nodding face that could not speak.

*

Andrew had brought Emily,
six years old,
who kept returning

to look at Jane, so still
in the silky coffin,
and the next day confided
to Alice Mattison,
"We saw Jane's actual body."

*

When Alice Ling finished
praying over Jane's coffin,
three hundred neighbors
and poets stood in spring
sunshine. Then Robert
started to sing "Amazing
Grace." Out of the silence
that followed he heard
his own voice saying,
"We have to go, dear."

*

That night he turned
his children out of the house
with difficulty, and was
alone again with her absence.
Before bed he drove
to the graveyard to say goodnight,
and at six A.M. dropped by
as if he brought her coffee.

*

Driving the highway, the day
after the funeral,
he felt suddenly overtaken
by a weight of shame
that reminded him of waking,
years ago in Ann Arbor,
knowing that the night
before, drunk, he had done
something despicable.

*

It was true, what he thought,
although pitiless. If he could say
now, "Jane has leukemia,"
he would feel such contentment.

*

In a nightmare that May,
Jane died in their house
far in a sunless forest.
The townspeople were sad
because she died
and because the sheriff
was coming to arrest him.
He had put out everything
of spirit and energy
taking care of Jane
and had neglected

the old women who starved
in their wooden cottages.

*

Saturday mornings he made
the same error again
and again. Writing Jane
letters at his desk,
he saw the clock at death's hour
and fell into tears. Wiping
his eyes he noted
that he mistook the time
and in sixty minutes
would need to howl again.

*

Every day he watched
the young green snake
on the granite step
by the porch's end
who sunned herself
in desolate noontime
and slipped like liquid
into her hole
after she lifted her head
to see his face.

*

For half a year at least
Jane's thick nearsighted
glasses lay on the table
by the bed, and the wristwatch
they bought at a jeweler's
in Rome on their sixteenth
anniversary — put there when
she could still see, when
what time it was mattered.

*

After a year he tried
to tell himself: Everyone
dies. Some die at three
days, and some
at forty-seven years.
How many have perished
in this long house,
or on the painted bed?
His grandmother and mother
were born in this place.
Only Jane's death
continues to prosper.

2

The Purpose of a Chair

When you look at a chair, it has a clear purpose: to be sat on. A spoon is for eating soup. Much of the time, when I consider what happens to us, it seems that the purpose of life is to suffer in agony and die.

—William Trout, *Last Notebooks*

AFTER HOMER

When I drove home
from Manchester Airport
after two nights
away, Jane ran out
from the screen door
with Gussie cavorting
behind her. I felt
like the wanderer
returning after twenty
years to his wife
and his dog.
        Stiff,
old, and alone,
I murder the suitors
all night each night
as they roister
in the stone hall.

BARBER

Jane's brush cut looked
like a Marine recruit's
as she sat skinny
and pale at the table,
interrupting our chore
to vomit in a china bowl.
We picked through jumbles
of medical supplies,
filling two garbage bags
with leukemia's detritus.
When I lifted up leftover
disinfectant or Duoderm,
she shook her head
no, and I tossed it away,
as I did with the Ziploc
of her massy hair,
cut off the year before
when it started to shed.
The young barber trembled.

Jane's last public outing
was our cousin Curtis's
funeral, dead at three days
in his mother's arms.
I carried a folding chair
and Jane held on tight
as we crept over ice
through the year's coldest
wind to the baby's hole.
Jane sat shaking, in tears,
pale and swaddled under down
and wool. Our neighbors
and cousins nodded, smiled,
and looked away. They knew
who would gather them next.

Her Intent

She concentrated her intent
on letting go. Florists' vans
pulled into the driveway four
or five times a day. I covered
the dining room table, kitchen
counters, and two cast-iron
Glenwoods with lilies
and bouquets of spring blossoms.
Jane wouldn't allow
roses or daisies or tulips
into the bedroom;
flowers and music were life.
I could not play her Messiaen,
nor Mendelssohn, nor *Black
and Blue*, nor Benita Valente
singing "Let Evening Come."

"I want," she said, "to tell you
something important. I want . . .
I want . . . spinach!" Angrily
she shook her head back and forth.
Eyesight departed after speech.

Retriever

Two days after Jane died
I walked with our dog Gus
on New Canada Road
under birchy green
April shadows, talking
urgently, trying
to make him understand.
A quick mink scooted past
into fern, and Gus
disappeared in pursuit.
The damp air grew chill
as I whistled and called
until twilight. I thought
he tried to follow her
into the dark. After an hour
I gave up and walked home
to find him on the porch,
alert, pleased to see me,
curious over my absence.
But Gus hadn't found her
deep in the woods; he hadn't
brought her back
as a branch in his teeth.

SWEATER

The second June afterward,
I wrapped Jane's clothes
for Rosie's Place
but I keep on finding
things I missed —
a scarf hanging from a hook
in the toolshed, a green
down vest, or a sweater
tossed on the swivel chair
by her desk where
her papers pile untouched,
just as she left them
the last time she fretted
over answering a letter
or worked to end a poem
by observing something
as careless as the white
sleeve of a cardigan.

ANOTHER CHRISTMAS

Our first Christmas together
at Eagle Pond I bought
a chainsaw to cut the tree
from our woodlot. Puffing
with accomplishment I set
an emaciated hemlock kitty-
corner from the Glenwood stove.

"What will become of Perkins?"
Jane asked when she could still
speak. Two years later
I miss her teasing voice
that razzed my grandiloquence:
"Perkins, dim your lights."
"Somebody cover Perkins's cage."

All year I could do anything
I wanted, any time of day
or night, travel anywhere, buy
anything. Therefore I sat
in my blue chair doing nothing
and trying to feel nothing.
On this second Christmas

I fix, decorate, and cherish
a visible vacancy kitty-
corner from the Glenwood.

Sometimes I dream awake.
Sometimes I see her face
in its strong-featured beauty
with her eyes full of pity.

Deathwork

Wake when dog whimpers. Prick
Finger. Inject insulin.
    Glue teeth in.
  Smoke cigarette.
    Shudder and fret.
Feed old dog. Write syllabic

On self-pity. Get *Boston Globe.*
Drink coffee. Eat bagel. Read
    At nervous speed.
  Smoke cigarette.
    Never forget
To measure oneself against Job.

Drag out afternoon.
Walk dog. Don't write.
    Turn off light.
  Smoke cigarette
    Watching sun set.
Wait for the fucking moon.

Nuke lasagna. Pace and curse.
For solitude's support
    Drink Taylor's port.
  Smoke cigarette.
    Sleep. Sweat.
Nightmare until dog whimpers.

The Perfect Life

Unicorns envy their cousin
horses a smooth forehead.
Horses weep for lack of horns.

Hills cherish the ambition
to turn into partial
differential equations,

which want to be poems, or dogs,
or the Pacific Ocean,
or whiskey, or a gold ring.

The man wearing the noose
envies an other who fondles
a pistol in a motel room.

Distressed Haiku

In a week or ten days
the snow and ice
will melt from Cemetery Road.

I'm coming! Don't move!

*

Once again it is April.
Today is the day
we would have been married
twenty-six years.

I finished with April
halfway through March.

*

You think that their
dying is the worst
thing that could happen.

Then they stay dead.

*

Will Hall ever write
lines that do anything
but whine and complain?

In April the blue
mountain revises
from white toward green.

*

The Boston Red Sox win
a hundred straight games.
The mouse rips
the throat of the lion

and the dead return.

Easters

On the first of the four Easters
she could still swallow, and six
days before death took her last
Communion. The tall young minister
prayed as if taking dictation
from a dying bloodstream.

On the second Easter I orbited
the world in a lust of quickness
that bloodied itself into rage
imagining murder, and collapsed
to despair. Nowhere among blasted
lilies could grace find an earth.

On the third Easter I sang hymns
and remembered earlier Aprils
when we gathered cold on the hill
at sunrise by Ansel and Edna's house,
ate homemade bacon and hot cross buns.
The grave remained the grave.

On the fourth Easter the passionate
minister with the face of a boy
spoke as he blessed Communion,
and my spirit lightened for the first
time since her death at the image
of a tomb opened, a hooded figure.

Now it is May: green hay, black flies,
and the returning peonies, each
year smaller without her attentions.
I visit her grave walking with Gus
but without ghosts; with daffodils,
carved names, and one year blank.

Throwing the Things Away

A mouse flitters across
the floor of the old parlor
and disappears among cartons.
On the carpet lie stacked
a thousand books,
acquired in excitement, now
given away unread. I find
a picture that hung
over the sofa for ten years,
and discover another cache
of Jane's dresses and jackets.
Here's an album of snapshots
she took in China.

*

           I open a box
that emptied a bureau drawer
in my mother's Connecticut
attic, and an intact day
from nineteen forty-two
leaps like a mouse surprised
eating a letter: a balsa
model of a Flying Fortress;
a ten-inch 78 of Connee
Boswell singing "The Kerry
Dancers"; a verse play,

The Folly of Existence;
the unbearable photographs
of young parents who cannot
know what will happen.
Exposed, a discovered body
crumbles into motes
revolving in deadly air.

*

By wavery piles of tapes and CDs,
near the TV, I find an electric
grinder, wedged in, labeled,
"To grind Indian spices *only.*"
Her underline. Why have I never
seen it, years after her death?
How did it get there? Maybe Jane
carried the grinder as the phone
rang, and set it down
to hear about bloodwork.

*

A friend
fills boxes of books to mail
to a Sioux reservation.
At a chest of drawers packed
with linen, she stands beside me
holding a trash bag. I lift
pillowcases, sheets, napkins,

doilies, and tablecloths,
and shake out weightless dry
housefly carcasses. Most
of the fabric is rotten or holey
or bloodstained. Sometimes
she says, "This one is hand
done. This one is old." We keep
the pretty pieces, fancywork
of farm women who sat at night
underneath the parlor's
kerosene lamp, their fingers
scuttling in the yellow light
as quick as mice.

*

        To the dump
with Bing Crosby and Dinah Shore,
with my mother's unfinished
tatting and her Agatha Christies.
To the dump with my father's
colorless Kodachrome slides
of their cross-country trip
together. To the dump
with bundles of linen
and the gooseneck lamp Jane
wrote poems by. To the dump
with the baseball and its eaten-
away glove, with my father,
dead forty years, with my mother

who lasted until ninety, with
Jane, with generations of mice,
with me — tidying, opening
boxes, throwing the things away.

ARDOR

Nursing her I felt alive
in the animal moment,
scenting the predator.
Her death was the worst thing
that could happen,
and caring for her was best.

After she died I screamed,
upsetting the depressed dog.
Now I no longer
address the wall covered
with many photographs,
nor call her "you"
in a poem. She recedes
into the granite museum
of JANE KENYON 1947–1995.

I long for the absent
woman of different faces
who makes metaphors
and chops onion, drinking
a glass of Chardonnay,
oiling the wok, humming
to herself, maybe thinking
how to conclude a poem.
When I make love now,
something is awry.

Last autumn a woman said,
"I mistrust your ardor."

This winter in Florida
I loathed the old couples
my age who promenaded
in their slack flesh
holding hands. I gazed
at young women with outrage
and desire—unable to love
or to work, or to die.

Hours are slow and weeks
rapid in their vacancy.
Each day lapses as I recite
my complaints. Lust is grief
that has turned over in bed
to look the other way.

3

Her Garden

. . .
Wind oozing thin through the thorn from norward
And the woman calling.

— Thomas Hardy, "The Voice"

Her Garden

I let her garden go.
    let it go, let it go
How can I watch the hummingbird
    Hover to sip
    With its beak's tip
The purple bee balm—whirring as we heard
    It years ago?

    The weeds rise rank and thick
    let it go, let it go
Where annuals grew and burdock grows,
    Where standing she
    At once could see
The peony, the lily, and the rose
    Rise over brick

    She'd laid in patterns. Moss
    let it go, let it go
Turns the bricks green, softening them
    By the gray rocks
    Where hollyhocks
That lofted while she lived, stem by tall stem,
    Dwindle in loss.

Hiding

I know she's gone for good,
I watched her die, but Gus is
Not sure. In the birch wood
He searches, looks, fusses.

When we walk home today
He sniffs at her armchair.
"She won't come back," I say.
He climbs an attic stair

And sticks his intent nose
Under a hamper's lid,
As if, for all he knows,
She slipped back in and hid.

Summer Kitchen

In June's high light she stood at the sink
    With a glass of wine,
And listened for the bobolink,
And crushed garlic in late sunshine.

I watched her cooking, from my chair.
    She pressed her lips
Together, reached for kitchenware,
And tasted sauce from her fingertips.

"It's ready now. Come on," she said.
    "You light the candle."
We ate, and talked, and went to bed,
And slept. It was a miracle.

Wool Squares

I sort through left-behind
    Boxes that keep
    A muddled heap
Of woman's work. I find
Wool squares she used to knit
While I sat opposite.

"Leftover life to kill,"
    Young Caitlin said
    With Dylan dead,
Yet lived with an ill will
Forty posthumous years
Of rage, fucking, and tears.

At seventy I taste
    In solitude
    Starvation's food,
As the land goes to waste
Where her death overthrew
A government of two.

Proctor Graveyard

With morbid joy we knew
That when we came to die
Our two bodies would lie,
First me, then you,
Four miles from Eagle Pond, under birch trees
For centuries
Fixed in the earth beneath an altering sky.

After the melt of snow,
From the black flies in June
Until leaves fall too soon,
The dog and I go
Walking among the graves, and stop at yours,
Where your mourners
Gathered themselves one April afternoon.

Burn the Album

The camera's click
Left us with snapshots of our picnic
Halfway up Kearsarge,
Perpetuating us
And the dog Gus.
Now one is grown, four others old,
And one is mold
In the Proctor graveyard underneath Kearsarge.

The album's pictures
Kill what they keep — nothing endures
Except Kearsarge —
As they preserve the way
We looked that day
Of beer and hotdogs, when we were
Prettier, younger,
And alive, picnicking halfway up Kearsarge.

The Touch

The months of absence hurry.
In sleep I touch her skin
And wake in the stain of dawn, in fury
Once more to know
It was her pillow
That mimicked the touch of a dead woman.

POND AFTERNOONS

When early July's
Arrival quieted the spring's black flies,
We spent green afternoons
Stretched on the moss
Beside dark Eagle Pond, and heard across
Its distances the calling of the loons.

The days swam by,
Lazy with slow content and the hawk's cry.
We lost ambition's rage,
Forgot it all,
Forgot Jane Kenyon, forgot Donald Hall,
And sleepily half glanced at a bright page.

Day after day
We crossed the flaking railroad tracks and lay
In the slant August sun
To nap and read
Beneath an oak, by the pond's pickerelweed.
Then acorns fell: These days were almost done.

Hours Hours

Mornings we wrote, in separate domains.
Midday we napped and loved, and rose from bed
Back to the desk or garden. Then we read
Aloud from James or Keats, my turn or Jane's.

Some days were rankled by the unforeseen.
I quarreled with a friend. Another died.
When things went wrong, I sighed, I paced and sighed,
Until we found our way back to routine.

In June the black flies stung as Eagle Pond did
When the sharp smarting light assailed our eyes
On afternoons of our old enterprise
When the twin solitudes still corresponded.

The Wish

I keep her weary ghost inside me.
"Oh, let me go," I hear her crying.
"Deep in your dark you want to hide me
And so perpetuate my dying.
    I can't undo
    The grief that you
Weep by the stone where I am lying.
    Oh, let me go."

By work and women half distracted,
I endure the day and sleep at night
To watch her dying reenacted
When the cold dawn descends like twilight.
    How can I let
    This dream forget
Her white withdrawal from my sight,
    And let her go?

Her body as I watch grows smaller;
Her face recedes, her kiss is colder.
Watching her disappear, I call her,
"Come back!" as I grow old and older,
    While somewhere deep
    In the catch of sleep
I hear her cry, as I reach to hold her,
    "Oh, let me go!"

III
DAYLILIES

Daylilies on the Hill 1975–1989

"Endurance is good," he said, "and best is the endurance
of magnitude." "Yes, yes," he answered, "of course:
centuries of cathedrals. On the other hand," he said,
"there is also the daylily."
                                                    Bees wake in May, roused
by the cry of lilac; skunkweed raises green hands;
July's fieldmice skitter in cornrows; in August

blackberries darken themselves on Acorn Hill as chilly
bees feel sleep arriving. At dawn in a warm drizzle,
June peas bush out beside lettuce leaves and asparagus,
old roses bud, and the goldfinch returns singing
as our dog Gus and I walk along Route 4 in first light,
no cars on the road. Fifteen hours later, we trudge again

through a cut hayfield, and twilight dew darkens my Nikes.
Fifty-five years ago I trimmed this field with a scythe,
pleasing my grandfather. To the west, foothills blacken
against a late sunset; overhead first stars. Branches
of dead elms fishbone up as empty in June as in January.
Two hundred years by the dirt turnpike, then by the blacktop,

they hoisted a magnanimous green. Now we set oak saplings
beside their stumps. Gus leaps at a moth, prances, and plumes
his gay tail high. Where we walk, the settlers' stone walls
square out old pasture. When I pace in the family house,
the layered past shows forth in two hundred years of things —
making house and land composite, alive and dead together.

In the back chamber, where we preserve broken beds and chairs,
tattery postcard albums, headless dolls, dolls' furniture,
wooden-runnered sleds, butter churns, spinning wheels,
and clocks without faces, three highchairs stand in a row.
The newest is Sears's fancy pressed oak from nineteen eleven,
mail-ordered when Nan was born, where I took my turn

in nineteen twenty-nine; beside it the wicker highchair
where my mother and two years later her sister Caroline
gummed their toast; alongside, another highchair, smaller
and older still, that fitted my grandmother Kate, born
in the north bedroom in eighteen seventy-eight.
                                        In February
seven-foot-deep snowfields will reflect a sky "as blue,"

my grandfather said, "as the seat of a Dutchman's pants."
When Gus leaps, running in snow, he will pause in the air
as if I dreamed him, and dry powder scatter in flurries
where he lands on the moondust snow.
                                  When we first
moved in, we looped cable around the tilting saphouse,
tied it to an eight-cylinder four-wheel-drive GMC pickup

and pulled it asunder. Under a collapsed cornerpost
we found two flat white rocks and turned them over: BENJAMIN
KENESTON 1789–1863. I remembered also his stone upright
in the old graveyard, where his son, BENJAMIN CILLEY KENESTON
1826–1913, raised it—after this one cracked and he carted
the pieces home to set under four-by-fours for the new saphouse

rising on the hill with its fresh-sawed, yellow-fibered planks.
    When the ice mountain receded thirty thousand years ago,
shedding gravel and boulders, leaving Eagle Pond behind
for the Penacook's trout, birds flew to the warming north
and shook seeds from their feathers to sprout in new dirt.
In the long drying, whippoorwills lay speckled eggs

and sang, and thrived on grubs and beetles for millennia,
but ten years of DDT concluded the whippoorwill race,
thinning shells until they fissured and embryos died.
Whippoorwills go out, go out—as if we watched house
lights go out, one by one, at night across the valley.
    Adding a new bathroom onto this old house, we sawed

through the irregular upright ash and cedar laths
of eighteen three. Light entered the dark mouse-precincts
long hammered shut, plastered and papered over almost
two centuries ago. We sawed through rough old boards
fastened by hand-forged nails over great sills of oak
hewn flat on two sides, and with their bark still clinging.

When we kindled a fire with wood two hundred years dry,
it blazed like kerosene.
                    In June's nine o'clock twilight—
rosegold over foothills, like copper showing through tin
linings of pots worn thin by generations in the same kitchen—
June plays its tune of mitosis. New leaf cells split, double,
and double again; green goes more green; Gus's nose

twitches at new buds in this hazy undersea dark. He sniffs,
waving his tail in dog-rapture at a flowering bush's base,
at rhubarb's rags, at the twiggy, new-set apple trees.
    Driving for the *Globe* at five o'clock on a warm morning,
I discover the store opened up like a rind, burned
out, black, smoke still rising from beams and timbers

heaped among hulks of coolers and freezers. One back wall
totters upright: on a standing shelf exploded cans. Wine
bottle shards glint in an alley behind a black cash register.
Volunteer firemen, who have worked all night to protect
house and barn, drink coffee and eat doughnuts provided
by the Ladies' Auxiliary. A dozen young men chew and sip,

wearing boots and bright slickers — exhausted, cheerful.
    Four kinds of baked beans, three casseroles of meatball stew,
salad, macaroni and cheese, Edna's red velvet cake, Ansel's
best rolls, Audrey's homemade ice cream: The Church
Fair copies itself every year, Julys turning into decades,
repeating, growing smaller, like the barber's mirrored wall.

    When I wake early morning in summer, I want to live
a hundred thousand days: The body's joy rises with dead
elms rising, black empty scaffolding alongside hayfields
under blue hills. Three crows as fat as roosters peck
at a coon killed on macadam: Yellow beaks rip on Route 4
in New Hampshire.
                    On a rainy day, by the light of one bulb,

picking again through the back chamber, we find a narrow
cardboard box with faint old-fashioned handwriting on it:
Wool sheared from B. C. Kenestons sheep   Carded
at Otterville   Ready for Spinning   April 1848.
  Next morning is fair again, and the mountain clear,
while mist rises from spiky hayfields cut last week.

  On the glorious Fourth of July in Andover, nineteen seventy-
six, we watched "Two Hundred Years of the Republic" parade: A girl
riding her shying horse; then the Bristol Shriners' band
wearing fezzes; then old cars, clowns, fire engines, one-wheelers,
oxen; then the floats of four churches, the Little League,
the 4-H Club, the Andover Volunteer Firemen, Future Farmers

of America, Boy Scouts, and the Rescue Squad—all fitted
to the theme "From Colony to Country." On the green, crafters
raised their stalls: fancywork, thrown pots, woodcuts, macramé.
After the baked beans and ham supper in the grade school
auditorium, we watched turtles race for the Lions; we threw
soggy baseballs at a target that, if we hit it, tumbled

a watery pailful on Sherman Buzzle, this glorious Fourth of July.
  Now I stand gazing while Gus searches out his tree
and lifts his leg abruptly against the ribbed bark of a stout
maple that I remember slim as a cornstalk fifty years ago.
I startle as overhead crows clamor *caw-caw-caw-caw-caw.*
  After Jane's daffodils go—before peonies and daylilies

rise red and yellow, before pink and white — overhead green
flaps broad flags from sugarbush, ash, birch, and oak
as it glories in the whole durable density of summer,
arrived in May, persistent through June rain, July heat,
August parch, and cool blue evenings of turning September,
departing into October's red.
                              Stone grows; stone extrudes

each spring as snow recedes from the fields. Stone's gravel,
crushed by engines or glaciers, becomes small boulders.
Stone's boulder hunkers huge by the roadside where the young horse
Riley shied at a shape that bulked like a revenant mammoth.
    Moments carve medallions — weeks, days, and hours — images
that mount themselves in the mind's permanent collection:

With Riley the old horse, my grandfather and I cut widow hay
July and August unrainy hot mornings forever; afternoons
we rake it together and fetch it home: timothy, fescue,
clover. As Riley turns his head to watch, twitching
green flies off his back, my grandfather Wesley pitches
forkfuls up, slow and steady. I build out stages of hay,

loading, between the rack's homemade split-pole rails.
Wesley works with the presence and practice of sixty years.
I watch him twist his fork in, balance, heave, balance,
and swing it over his head: so, so . . .
                              By the kitchen
window, under the canary, in many incarnations always
named Christopher, that preened in December singing yellow,

my grandmother Kate braided her long hair, looking south
toward dawn. She planned her day: Monday washing, Tuesday
ironing, Wednesday baking, Thursday cleaning . . . She made
soap twice a year; she darned socks, sewed buttons and seams,
crocheted and tatted after supper each night; she churned pale
butter once a week, put hens' and pullets' eggs down

in waterglass midsummer, and each morning under Christopher's
cage observed with gratitude: "Mountain's real pretty today."
    Every day I carve these images of Wesley and Kate,
making reliefs or intaglios from summers more than fifty
years ago. This year as an old man I remember
the old people of this house. Last night I woke from sleep

seeing again the generous faces of Wesley and Kate.
    The eagle my great-grandfather knew fished this pond night
and morning, single bird who kept house on Eagle's Nest.
Our forty acres of cold water gathered under borders
of birch, hemlock, and oak to breed pickerel, horned pout,
minnows, sunfish, trout, and perch.
                            Maybe I was eight or nine;

my grandfather hitched Riley to the buggy's shafts;
my grandmother took off her apron and pinned her hat.
Riley labored up New Canada Road to the Dobbins place
for the auction — a social rally, like Old Home Day
or the Fourth, or Uncle Luther's annual surprise birthday
party each August twenty-first. Freeman was there, his beard

wagging around his permanent smile as he talked without stopping.
My grandmother's old schoolmate Lucille turned up
to gossip with: Who's bedridden? Who's next to die?
I met my grandfather's old friend Merrill Huntoon,
blind, who pitched for Danbury while my grandfather
played second base. Peddlers' barrows at the crowd's

edge sold tonic, ice cream, Rawleigh's Salve, and Quaker Oil.
When the auctioneer banged his gavel we stopped talking.
Gradually I understood what was auctioned off. For the first
time I heard the dead lament their characteristic loss.
After Belle died, Victor couldn't keep the house alone,
and my grandfather gave him a bite of land for a shack.

Mr. Hall from Hill lifted up stuff for folks to bid on:
Ball jars by the dozen, a pram, apple peelers, old boots,
chairs, tables, quilts, feather pillows and mattresses,
boxes of pretty pictures (snipped-off Christmas cards,
pastels of babies cut from magazines, daguerreotypes
of matriarchs, bearded fathers and Civil War boys, dressed-

up daughters), a Shaker basket, hammers, saws, a level,
oil lamps, heavy wooden skis, diaries, pedal sewing machines
—whole lives of the dead going, gone, for a nickel or a dime.
    On these summer nights, after Gus and I walk, I swivel
a satellite dish and materialize the Boston Red Sox
to get sleepy by, watching a few innings from Baltimore

or Fenway Park. A visitor from Boston pretends outrage:
"*What* would your grandfather think?" I imagine Wesley Wells,

after milking and locking up the hens, sitting to watch
Ted Williams or Nomar. He grins with pleasure, snorts
at failure, and, drowsy after five innings, goes to bed.
   In eighteen sixty my great-great-grandfather complained:

"Now, your modern inventions are just fine, like this railroad,
but . . . when I was a boy the twelve-horse teams carted
loads of ash for the hame shop, or grain for Johnson's mill.
You never *saw* such horses." Today I walk in a sandy trench;
small trees grow between ties over the yellowed stone
I remember new and white in wartime fifty years ago.

Hayfields shuddered with freight; sheep turned slow heads
at tremors of tonnage, war's iron rolling. When we heard
the four A.M. freight, we knew: one more hour on feathers.
   In September dawn, cold dew shines on hayfields. By noon
the still-tall sun brings back July: blue sky, a warm breeze
that wavers the pond's turning birches. I wait for the branch

that reddens first each year by Chester Ludlow's house:
Then swamp maples carmine; then the whole clamor and glory.
   The fire that never went out went out in the range
where strongest coffee dripped winter and summer, where berries
boiled or cold-packed darkened blue Ball jars, where a reservoir
heated water for washing dishes, where home-rendered lard melted

to fry doughnuts, where the tough setting-hen boiled four hours
into fricassee, where the bread baked twelve loaves at once,
and mince pies and custard. While this fire went out, elsewhere
damp fire burned slowly in sills two hundred years old, and ants

carried oak away consonant by consonant. Now as the range
sits in all weathers behind the toolshed — beside mowing machine,

whittled ladder, bullrake, and pitchfork — its black cast iron
burns itself down in the fire of rust that never goes out.
                                                        No cars
on Route 4 tonight, so Jane and I walk on the macadam. Gus pulls
as we keep to the white gutter line, visible in starlight
beside glacial New Hampshire sand. No sound as we turn back
except for the chill tinkling of dog license and rabies tag.

Ahead, the single porchlight projects its yellow oblong
over black grass interrupted by trees. When Gus pauses
to sniff, his pale tail waves like ectoplasm under a sky
without moon or clouds, crazed by the ten million stars
I number by actual count this darkest autumn night.
    It must have been Ben Keneston who made this door

in eighteen sixty-five when he added a shed and a woodshed
to the old Cape he bought to move into with his family,
and hung it between shed and woodshed. He nailed five
vertical boards against two across. Shiny, ridged and scored,
never painted, the door shows scallops of wear on top
and bottom. To keep it shut against the open woodshed —

against Gypsies and Frenchmen — he chiseled an oblong latch,
two inches by five, out of rock maple to swivel on a bolt
fastened to the jamb, with a thumb of wood nailed underneath
and a spike dangling from twine to fit a hole above it.
The same spike hangs from the seventeenth length of twine.
This hardened latch — dark brown, solid, with little bumps

and hollows like a turnip's — wood that turns pages in the book
of connections, wood touched ten thousand times by dozens
of hands — shines like Saint Peter's toe.

Warm rain in the morning:
Gus stretches, yawns, mutters, and remembers to mark his maple.
As I drive to town for the paper, headlights on at five-thirty,
wipers swoop against cool drizzle, repeating themselves.

I pass the burnt store, half cleared away, the dank air
still thick with creosote.

We drive late on a night
of ripe sweetcorn in blithe air, tomatoes ripening. By Route 11
our headlights immobilize a family of five raccoons, pirates
of corn conspiring, bright eyes glinting.

At Christian Endeavor
young Edna led us, her face passionate with goodness and humor,

as we sang Sunday night hymns early in the nineteen forties.
Because I loved trains, I raised my hand every week to sing
"Life Is Like a Mountain Railroad," and every week we sang
Edna's favorite, which Fred played again on a bright day
as we carried Edna from the South Danbury Christian Church,
where she spent the Sundays of seventy-two years, in a box

with bronze handles to the long car and the Danbury graveyard,
Ansel standing in silence — : "I come to the garden alone
while the dew is still on the roses."

Uncle Luther remembered
the Civil War. As he sat on the sunny porch, in the captain's
chair where his father lived out his last summer,
I asked him questions. I was nine, aware that Luther would die,

who remembered a countryside busy with young men and women.
He let me see how decades lapsed, the people packed up
and departed, weeds grew, and the wooden houses tilted inward
to collapse into cellarholes. Stories continue as the earth
continues. And the best way to preserve topsoil, as the man said,
is to pave it over: Do I pave it over by writing it down?

Do I glass it in?
      I sat by my grandfather's side at church;
He wore a brown suit from my father's closet as Luther preached
his sermon without notes. Above the pump organ my grandmother
Kate's black sequined hat tossed as she played "Rock of Ages,
cleft for me." When we stood for a hymn I saw her mouth
a great O. If I wriggled, my grandfather's Sunday

face looked down, and his right hand fumbled in his pocket
to fetch me a Canada Mint.
      On March third last year, the sap moon
disappeared behind clouds, wind rose, the temperature dropped,
and in the morning four inches of fresh snow covered
the disgrace and ruin of the yard where Sherman's snowplough
tormented turf. Snow recovered its scabby layers on hayfields.

By noontime sun dazzled from new snow as the air warmed.
Therefore in the hills today, under old snow and new, maple trunks
three hundred years old start their yearly work. If tonight
freezes, tomorrow's sun will release sweetness into our buckets.
  An elm by the road—taller than the house, four feet thick,
two hundred years old—leans ripping and creaking as the saw

tears it through. It poises, its topmost branches trembling
as it starts to sag, lowering slowly, sliding and tearing,
inch by inch, tilting, leaning, groaning, until the trunk
shreds its last fibers loose and streaks through shocked air
to strike the ground bouncing its great stiff length out—
and settles still.
                    In March, the melt fissures snowfields

that hover detached from hillsides beside ditches where water
runs day and night without pausing. Gray layers that remain
on hayfields must have fallen last year in December.
This ancient snow lay where it fell all winter, diminishing
in January's thaw or as the determining moon circled
toward this moment of melt. Now, underneath a damp vanishing

lid, woodchucks sleep without stirring toward spring.
Or maybe a restless one knocks on the underside of the snow.
    This photograph—in the fold-down desk my grandmother earned
with coupons from Larkin's Soap, after she stopped making
her own soap—shows an old woman in a Mother Hubbard
beside a bearded man next to their middle-aged children

as shiny as boiled eggs, and in front a young mother who holds
a baby feathered in lace. The baby in the photograph
married, bore nine children, had twenty-five grandchildren,
buried two husbands, survived ten years alone, broke her hip,
and was buried in the graveyard under a granite marker
that carves her name and the dates of her life. Maybe . . .

I do not know her name.
                                    Daylilies rise from the hill.
The structure persisted against assaults of poverty, hurricanes,
education, ignorance, money, Massachusetts, automobiles, war,
drought, secession, fire, flood, and the closing mills.
Now it sickens of outnumbering as the Nashua developer builds
seventy houses on Dobbins Hill.
                                    Morning and night now, Gus and I

walk past blond elm stumps cut close to the ground, smoothed off
by a highway crew. Gus meditates ruin. Daylilies
collapse on the hill; asters return; maples redden again
as summer departs again. When we stroll the Pond Road
at nightfall, western sun stripes down through dust
raised by the yellow pickup passing five minutes ago:

vertical birches, hilly road, sunlight slant and descending.

IV
Ardor

The Old Lover

He climbs slowly through ferns
a mile to the high pasture
where the sun on the bright
grass is the skin's rapture,

as great as a baby's, who
whoops, gurgles awake in his crib,
and flaps his arms and legs,
lusty and loud as a rooster.

Conversation's Afterplay

At dinner our first night
I looked at you, your bright green eyes,
In candlelight.
We laughed and told the hundred stories,
Kissed, and caressed, and went to bed.
"Shh, shh," you said,
"I want to put my legs around your head."
Green eyes, green eyes.

At dawn we sat with coffee
And smoked another cigarette
As quietly
Companionship and eros met
In conversation's afterplay,
On our first day.
Late for the work you love, you drove away.
Green eyes, green eyes.

CHARITY AND DOMINION

As we lay together after,
my forefinger modeled
your fair strong cheekbones
and you took my thumb
into your mouth, sucking it
carefully, licking its tip.

Tickle the trembling skin
of an arm or a leg
and even the little
skin hairs keep on coming.

I understood your charity
and dominion. I felt
like a fish flapping
on a boat's deck, and gasped
to the pretty stranger,
"I almost want to say that
I love—" You shook your head
fiercely and burst out:
"But it would be a lie!"

I admired your resolve,
your redeeming conviction
that rapture was trivial,
as you laughed all night
like a milkmaid in a meadow,
petticoats flung upward.

Razor

You sat in the booth
across from me in shadow
and your wide brown eyes
softened and flared
as you spoke remembering
the sickly adored
father of your girlhood —
how you brought him tea
and his newspaper, how
you stood beside him
while he shaved, your head
as high as the washbowl,
and lathered your face
the way he did, and shaved
using your little finger
as a Gillette Safety Razor.

Your voice in an ardor
of old tenderness
lightened the darkness
of the bar at midnight.
You pigtailed my hair
and in your room rubbed
moisturizer from a jar
to smooth my wrinkles.

BUOYANCY

1

When I undid the clasp of your bra
and your soft breasts toppled
against my chest, I thought
of Italian pears deliberately
chosen from barrows, those
cathedrals of fruit in October,
to be bitten into after bread
and dolce latte, drenchingly
wet with the first bite.

2

I showed you the unpainted barn
and felt your body grow tense
beside me. I had forgotten
what happened in a hayloft,
where the man who juggled three
eggs riding a unicycle raped
his six-year-old stepdaughter,
and motes in the dry air spun
slow globes of hurt and shame.

3

In August sunlight we lay
on soft thick moss by the pond.
When we walked into the dark
water up to our shoulders,

you took off your suit and pulled
mine down. What overflowing
comfort as we rose and fell
in the body's restitution, absorbed
by the careless resolve of water.

"MAISON D'AUJOURD'HUI"

The night refills itself.
Limestone drops to the sea
that varies blue all day
between capes that curve
like a lover's arms
to hold the tranquil waters.
Here on a stone bench
we watch the darkening
bay, its almost-still soft
skin. This morning
we drove among rock
villages and orchards
to visit Matisse's Chapel
with its carnal blues
and yellows. Underneath
our room an olive's
roots draw virgin oil
from the earth's body,
surging upward to leaves
silvery green and dark.
After siesta we throbbed
with the olive's thrust
and our bodies floated
as buoyant as the sea
that rolls inside us
tonight. Our joyous
flesh sighs, every cell

breathing, alert
to storeys of pastel
stucco with tile roofs
and filigreed balconies,
to the setting sun
that toplights with gold
a Mediterranean cloud.
Last night we wept, knowing
that nothing will last.
Now we sit idle, content
from breath to breath
in the house of today.
Across from our bench
a woman in a long black
smock closes the shutters
of her pink façade.

Impossible Lovers

1

When the clothes fell away
from your caryatid body
—stone become dancer's
modeled flesh—you clutched
me in, your small face
distorted as if in agony.

In the kitchen you cooked
risotto, moving surely
in your tall body, your neck
bent over the skillet,
your brown eyes scrupulous,
intent on making dinner.

2

What a season. Never in the old stories
of witches and gold coins did the air
breed dragons as it did all summer.

On the coast in August the sun never set.
Our twinges were scholarly twinges
like the twist of your studious mouth.

You called me god; I admitted it freely.
You were Aphrodite costumed in skin.
I was Zeus in the guise of a graybeard.

3

I sat in my chair opposite you, looking
at the curve of your thigh as smooth
as a sandbank, your long nimble legs
twisted beneath you.

                    Our hips
just touched as we slept all night,
making one body and one dreamer
although we were impossible lovers,
because we were impossible lovers.

The Peaceable Kingdom

Rarely did your toenails
scrape the ceiling, and only twice
did you dial 911 when my nightcap
concussed against plaster
— or maybe a rainforest's
canopy? You wore a furpiece.
Sometimes our red fitted
sheets maneuvered
to embrace us like pythons,
but I growled and roared,
becoming a lion,
and the snakes slithered behind
the headboard — or was it
the headwaters of the Nile?
You squeezed to wring
ultimate convulsions
from a stainless tusk quilted
with nerves. Thrusts
and inductions were multiple
and fierce, as if a rhinoceros
mated with a wildebeest,
unmaking the veldt, leaving
scratches on the horizon.

SUN

Both of us felt it: That day was an island,
strewn with rocks and lighthouses and lovers,
in the generous ocean. On the mainland,
people went about their business, eating
the *Times*, glancing through coffee and oatmeal,
as we walked the gangway into an original dream
of attentiveness, as if a day's pleasure
could concentrate us as much as suffering,
as if the seawall were a banquet without
surfeit, as if we could walk hand in hand
with no one nearby, as if silence and blue
wind became an Atlantic cove to float in,
and the air centered itself in small purple
butterflies flitting among the weed flowers.
In the darkening city we returned to,
our privacy completed the cafés of strangers.

Villanelle

Katie could put her feet behind her head
Or do a grand plié, position two,
Her suppleness magnificent in bed.

I strained my lower back, and Katie bled,
Only a little, doing what we could do
When Katie tucked her feet behind her head.

Her torso was a C-cup'd figurehead,
Wearing below its navel a tattoo
That writhed in suppleness upon the bed.

As love led on to love, love's goddess said,
"No lovers ever fucked as fucked these two!
Katie could put her feet behind her head!"

When Katie came she never stopped. Instead,
She came, cried "God!," and came, this dancer who
Brought ballerina suppleness to bed.

She curled her legs around my neck, which led
To depths unplumbed by lovers hitherto.
Katie could tuck her feet behind her head
And by her suppleness unmake the bed.

LOVE POEM

When I fall in love,
I jockey my horse
into the flaming barn.

I hire a cabin
on the shiny *Titanic*.
I tease the black bear.

Reading the *Monitor*,
I scan the obituaries
looking for my name.

DREAD AND DESIRE

The body's adversaries
salt the pink filet
of concupiscence.
When the woman desired
changes her shape
and the rotten oaks
grow up from stumps
to fall again, ardor
floods the Dakotas
of subject and object.
I want, I want, I *want*
to rub my wrinkles
against smooth skin.

Out of Bed

They remove themselves, one after one, leaving
behind them hair ties, the yellow of love,
and salt abandonment. I become as sheer
as the wave's bell and as redundant. Returned
from the sexual sea I achieve degradation:
the overturned boat, blue hands clutching,
an angry tongue that specifies the drowned.

AFFIRMATION

To grow old is to lose everything.
Aging, everybody knows it.
Even when we are young,
we glimpse it sometimes, and nod our heads
when a grandfather dies.
Then we row for years on the midsummer
pond, ignorant and content. But a marriage,
that began without harm, scatters
into debris on the shore,
and a friend from school drops
cold on a rocky strand.
If a new love carries us
past middle age, our wife will die
at her strongest and most beautiful.
New women come and go. All go.
The pretty lover who announces
that she is temporary
is temporary. The bold woman,
middle-aged against our old age,
sinks under an anxiety she cannot withstand.
Another friend of decades estranges himself
in words that pollute thirty years.
Let us stifle under mud at the pond's edge
and affirm that it is fitting
and delicious to lose everything.

Library of Congress Cataloging-in-Publication Data

Hall, Donald, date.
The painted bed / Donald Hall.
p. cm.
ISBN 0-618-18789-8
ISBN 0-618-34075-0 (pbk.)
I. Title.

PS3515.A3152 P35 2002
811'.54—dc21   2001051620

A number of poems previously appeared, in earlier versions, in the following publications: *American Poetry Review:* Charity and Dominion; Dread and Desire; Impossible Lovers; The Peaceable Kingdom; Out of Bed. *The American Scholar:* Another Christmas. *Arts & Letters:* Easters; Love Poem. *The Atlantic Monthly:* Distressed Haiku; Razor. *Between the Lines:* Throwing the Things Away. *Café Review:* Buoyancy. *CCNY:* Retriever. *Double-Take:* Hours Hours. *Five Points:* Throwing the Things Away. *Gettysburg Review:* Kill the Day. *Iowa Review:* The After Life; Her Intent. *The Literary Imagination:* The Wish. *Maine Times:* Folding Chair; Retriever. *Meridian:* Barber. *Michigan Quarterly Review:* Daylilies on the Hill 1975–1989; Wool Squares (formerly "Old Song"). *The New Republic:* Deathwork. *The New Yorker:* Affirmation; Ardor; Conversation's Afterplay (formerly "Conversation"); The Painted Bed (formerly "Words from the Sarcophagus"); The Perfect Life; Sun; Villanelle. *Oxford Today:* After Homer; Sweater. *The Sewanee Review:* Burn the Album; Proctor Graveyard. *Slate:* Summer Kitchen. *Times Literary Supplement:* Her Garden; Pond Afternoons; Retriever. *Tin House:* Her Garden; Pond Afternoons; The Touch. *The Warwick Press:* Summer Kitchen. *Witness:* The Old Lover (formerly "Geriatric Eros").

The After Life and The Purpose of a Chair also appeared in *The Purpose of a Chair*, a fine-press edition printed and bound by Sam and Sally Green at the Brooding Heron Press, Waldron Island, Washington.

DONALD HALL is the author of numerous books of poetry and prose, including the poetry collection *Without* and the story collection *Willow Temple*. He has received the National Book Critics Circle Award and the Los Angeles Times Book Prize for *The One Day*, the Lenore Marshall Award for *The Happy Man*, the Frost Medal from the Poetry Society of America for *Old and New Poems*, and the Ruth Lilly Poetry Prize. He was recently honored with the President's Award from the New England Booksellers Association. A member of the American Academy of Arts and Letters, he lives in New Hampshire.